Joan of Arc:
I Am Not Afraid

www.AWAKESTORIES.com

Joan of Arc: I Am Not Afraid

by Tara Mayoros

Illustrated by Todd Powelson

Published by Awake Stories, LLC

About Awake Stories

Our Creator has endowed us with certain unalienable Rights, among them are Life, Liberty, and the pursuit of Happiness. Through telling the stories of historical figures we enlighten, entertain, and educate people on these Rights.

Our short books and videos explore what molded people of the past into the extraordinary individuals they became.

We invite you to join us in unraveling the rich tapestry of the past and to find inspiration for you and your family.

Free Resources

Did you know that each of our books has a companion short film on our website? We also have study guides, video podcasts, artwork and even music available to help you further learn about these historical figures.

Simply go to our website address shown and enter your email address to access these amazing FREE resources.

https://www.awakestories.com/joanofarc/

ACKNOWLEDGEMENTS

The author and team members at Awake Stories, LLC would like to thank our amazing collaborators, which include: our actors, actresses, make-up artists, set designers, narrators, editors, guest talent, and our families.
Thank you for your love and support.

Where real-life historical figures appear, the situations, incidents, and dialogues concerning those persons are based loosely on historical events and are not intended to depict actual events. In all other respects, any resemblance to actual persons, living or dead, events, or locales is entirely coincidental.

No part of this publication and illustrations within may be reproduced, stored in a retrieval system, or transmited in any form or by any means, electronic, mechanical, photocopying, recording, or otherwise, without the prior written permission of Awake Stories, LLC.

Cover design by Steve Vistaunet.
Text copyright ©2024 by Tara Mayoros.
Illustrations copyright ©2024 by Todd Powelson.
All rights reserved. Awake Stories, LLC.

10 9 8 7 6 5 4 3 2 1

Printed in the United States of America

Contents

Introduction ix

Chapter One 1

Chapter Two 5

Chapter Three 9

Chapter Four 13

Chapter Five 17

Chapter Six 21

Chapter Seven 27

Chapter Eight 33

Chapter Nine 39

Chapter Ten 43

Chapter Eleven 47

Apply What You Learned 49

Film Notes 51

Joan of Arc Timeline 58

Timeline of World Events 59

References and Notes 60

Introduction

From the very moment I first encountered her powerful words, "I am not afraid, I was born to do this," Joan of Arc has stood as a monumental heroine in my life. Her resolute battle cry has served as a clarion call during moments of doubt, fear, and trials.

The exploration of Joan's life has become an integral part of my own journey, with her profound quote resonating with me since the very age she spoke those words. It was only natural for Joan of Arc to be one of the first historical figures to captivate my attention. To convey her remarkable story, the talents of artist Todd Powelson chose to depict her life through images reminiscent of stained glass. This choice felt fitting as I traced Joan's footsteps in France through her paper trail, numerous statues, and the captivating stained glass narratives scattered across the stunning landscapes. It brings me great joy to witness that she continues to be honored, remembered, and even venerated as a patron saint of France.

Beyond being a figure to admire from afar, Joan of Arc's unwavering faith, determination, and grit serve as more than golden statues adorning the crowded streets and cathedrals of Paris and

France. Her life, particularly her unjust demise, serves as a profound example for us all—to stand true to our convictions, even when confronted by seemingly insurmountable opposition. Joan's legacy, immortalized in art and history, is a timeless reminder of the strength that can be found in staying true to one's beliefs in the face of adversity.

Chapter One

On the eastern edge of France, in the quaint little town of Domrémy, lived a young girl named Jehanne d'Arc. During her nineteen years of life, she would take on several other names: Jeanne la Pucell (Joan the maid), La Pucell d'Orléans (the Maid of Orleans), the Maid of God, and the name by which she is most well-known today—Joan of Arc.[1]

Joan was born in 1412 to peasant farmers Jacques d'Arc and Isabelle Romée. The family, which included Joan's three brothers and a sister, worked nearly thirty acres of land in the village. Joan learned domestic skills and was very helpful around her home and village.[2] Isabelle was a pious woman who taught Joan to pray and passed down a tradition and expectation of religious devotion. Joan was often reminded to pray by the ringing of the church bells, which were within earshot of their home. The chiming bells marked time but also sounded alerts when enemies were within striking distance of Domremy, something that could happen at any moment in that tumultuous period.

Often seen in a red, wool-spun dress, Joan could be found working and playing in the woods and fields near her home. She grew to be strong and thoughtful, hardworking, and devoted.

The freedom she might have felt in those fields as a young child, however, stood in stark contrast to the red stains of war that marked the surrounding lands. Joan likely listened to the worry of her neighbors and parents and felt the strain of living in an area full of conflict.

Chapter Two

At the time of Joan's birth, France had been mired for seventy-five years in a long-running war with England. The conflict, which would later come to be known as the Hundred Years' War, had left her country torn apart by decades of bloodshed, starvation, and death. At the heart of the conflict was the question of who could rightfully claim the French throne.

With the death of King Charles IV in 1328, the French throne sat empty because Charles had no sons and no living brothers. His sister, Isabella (wife to Edward II of England), believed that her son, Edward III, should claim the throne for England. This, of course, enraged the French patrician class, who insisted the throne pass to Philip VI, Count of Valois and Charles's patrilineal first cousin.[3] A decision by the ruling French court gave the throne to Philip, who ruled for a tenuous nine years, until Edward challenged the claim, and a long, bloody war ensued.

The greedy hands of war claimed the lives of many people in the hundred years that followed. By the fall of 1428, France was on the precipice of destruction. England—aided by French Burgundians who were not loyal to the

Valois line—had already laid claim to the southwestern coast of France, and only one city stood between its army and central France: Orléans. In a series of calculated attacks, English troops commandeered the land surrounding the city, essentially trapping its residents inside in a ploy to let Orléans fall on its own as the confined townspeople surrendered to famine and hopelessness. By the spring of 1429, the English army could taste victory, and the people of Orléans were, indeed, without hope—starving, exhausted, and desperate for a miracle.

Chapter Three

Some 260 kilometers away from Orléans, in Domrémy, that miracle was taking form. Four years earlier young Joan had begun experiencing heavenly visions in the fields near her home. In the beginning, the saints who appeared in these visions had encouraged Joan to lead a devout life. The archangel, Saint Michael, called to her, saying, "Joan, do not be afraid. I am here to help you. Be a good girl, obey your parents, and God will help you."[4] Over time, the visions had become more vivid, and she could easily discern the saints who visited her. In addition to Saint Michael, she also saw Saint Catherine of Alexandria, who had been martyred 1,100 years earlier, and Saint Margaret of Antioch.

In 1428, when Joan was sixteen, the angelic voices grew more urgent. Catherine of Alexandria said to her, "Your people are starving. You must ensure the Dauphin becomes the king of France. You will know his face when you see him. You must liberate your people and lead France to victory."

Saint Margaret urged, "Go. We will be with you always if you keep your promise of being good and virtuous."

Although frightened by these heavenly visitors at first, Joan eventually came to trust their voices, to believe that she had been called to leave Domrémy, find the future king—a man she'd never laid eyes on—and advise him on how to defeat the English invaders.

Chapter Four

By February 1429, the people trapped in Orléans were near their breaking point, and Joan was on a mission to save them—and to save France. Now seventeen, Joan had gained a following of people who believed angels spoke with her and that God was using her to save France. She was becoming a living symbol of hope. With an armed escort of six men and her honorable reputation preceding her, Joan made her way from Domrémy to a castle in Chinon to meet Charles the VII, Dauphin of France.

Upon arriving at the castle, Joan strode confidently into a hall filled with three hundred knights. She walked with purpose through a doubtful crowd, looking intently at all the faces. A man dressed in fine clothing approached; some pointed to him, saying he was the Dauphin.[5]

"You are not the Dauphin," she said, turning in the candlelight to get a better view of the man's face. "Why do you seek to trick me?"

She continued to weave through the throng of people, searching for the Dauphin, her frustration growing. But then she saw him; she knew in an instant it was him. Against the stone walls, somewhat hidden behind the crowd, was a man dressed in simple clothing.

As she approached him, the true Dauphin, she heard the voices of her saints confirming his identity. A light gleamed on his face, and she knelt down.

"Gentle Dauphin, I have come to you on a message from God, to bring help to you and to your kingdom."[6]

She took his hand and kissed it. The crowd gasped in unison. Truly this miracle had come from heaven, for the crowd had tried very hard to trick her and thus expose her as a fraud.[7]

Chapter Five

Unlike the future king, some did not believe Joan was a messenger from God or that she could in any way help save France. Many of the Dauphin's counselors, political leaders, and priests wanted proof that God was speaking through her. From Chinon, the Dauphin took Joan to Poitiers, where many of France's scholars and theologians had retreated during the long English invasion. For several weeks in Poitiers,

Joan was questioned about her devoutness, her virtue, and the voices she heard. Her impatience grew with every question, for she knew that time delayed meant further death and devastation for her people. The voices she heard had told her she would lead an army to Orléans, and she intended to do just that.

"In God's name!" she said, "I am not come to show signs in Poitiers; but lead me to Orleans and I will show you the signs for which I am sent."[8]

Finally, Joan gained the trust of the counselors and of the church. They now believed that denying her request to command soldiers would be denying an order from heaven itself. And so, with the help and support of the Dauphin—who would shortly become King Charles VII—Joan was given an army.

A series of miracles began to happen in rhythm, as if the drums of her dedicated soldiers could be heard all the way to the heavens.

Before Joan had come to Chinon, she had cut her hair and dressed in the clothes of a man to draw less attention to her travel and eventual entrance to the royal court.[9] To look the part now, and to show her commitment to her troops—and to God—Joan again trimmed her hair and dressed like a man, riding into battle looking no different from the soldiers who rode behind her.

Chapter Six

There was much for Joan to do as she prepared for battle. Almost immediately, she learned the art of riding and maneuvering a stalwart war horse. For physical protection, an incredible suit of armor was made and paid for by the French people. The armor was fitted to her exact measurements. At the time, it was essentially unheard of to have armor made for a woman.

Next, she needed a sword. From the voice of Saint Catherine, Joan learned of a sword hidden behind the altar at the church in Sainte-Catherine-de-Fierbois. The voice told her that the sword would not be buried very deep. It would be "rusted, with five crosses engraved on it," but when the steel was touched, the old rust would fall away and expose a magnificent hilt and blade. Miraculously, the sword's retrieval happened just as Joan said it would. The old sword was recovered, rubbed clean of the rust that covered it, and presented to her.[10] Joan believed God would never have her kill anyone but that she should sharpen the weapon's blade notwithstanding and nobly carry it into the battles that would follow.

The final addition to Joan's battle attire was her banner, or standard.

The Lord's messengers had told Joan to take up the banner of the Lord, and so she had a banner made, sown with fleurs-de-lis and depicting two angels on either side of God, who was shown holding the world in his hands. On the fringed, silk banner were written the names of Jesus and Mary.[11]

One purpose of the banner was to indicate a precise location where Joan's army could regroup. On several occasions, when her troops were losing ground and lost in confusion on the battlefield, Joan would ride into the midst of battle, using her banner to mark her position on the field and rally her men on to victory.

"I would prefer, maybe forty times, my standard to my sword," Joan would later testify. "I carried my standard in my own hand when we went to the assault, to avoid having to kill anyone. I have never killed anyone."[12]

Chapter Seven

With her magnificent armor, sword, and banner, the young girl Joan led an army of four thousand men to Orléans. As they fought for the besieged city, Joan became a most unusual warrior who prayed for her enemies and even tried to help their wounded. She prohibited her soldiers from plundering for food, using strong drink, and fighting on the Sabbath.

One evening, after a victorious battle on a fortified area just outside Orléans, Joan told the army's chaplain, Jean Pasquerel, to keep close to her during the next day's battle, "for tomorrow I will have much to do, more than I have ever done before; and tomorrow blood will leave my body above my breast."[13]

The next day, as Joan was climbing a ladder she'd set against an English-occupied stone tower, she was pierced by an arrow and fell to the ground.

She thrashed around in pain, then reached for the arrow at her shoulder, just above her breast. She heard the clanging of swords, war, and soldiers shouting in the distance.

"Fall back! Fall back! She's hurt," yelled some of the soldiers.

Joan herself pulled out the arrow, and blood spurted onto the ground. The wound was packed with olive oil and bacon fat to stop the bleeding. Some suggested a spell or charm be given to help her, but Joan declared, "I would prefer to die rather than to do something I know to be a sin, or against the will of God."[14]

Slowly, with extra labor, she reached down and grabbed her banner with her good hand, clenching her other hand over her wound.

"Courage! Do not fall back," she yelled in a commanding voice. "In a little the place will be yours. Watch! when you see the wind blow my banner against the bulwark, you shall take it."[15]

It was mid-day, and as the battle raged on, Joan was carried away from the fighting by one of her loyal soldiers. She went to pray and to rest. That evening, she returned with determination and strength.

She stood tall, silhouetted against the heavenly rays of the falling sun shining upon her armor. Her banner waved high into the sky as she gave the French soldiers courage. "All is yours!" Joan cried, touching her banner to the nearest tower. "Enter!"

Rallied by Joan's strength and faith, the French were, at last, victorious. The English retreated from Orléans, leaving the city free. The French, with Joan at the helm, reentered the city, where they were met with praise and parading.

Chapter Eight

Her intent to unite the French under one king was at last in sight. Just two months after victory at Orléans, Charles VII was crowned king of France. Joan had followed the celestial voices and fulfilled her divine responsibilities. In the ensuing months, she would lead her army to a number of victories, causing hope to burn brighter than it had in years.

But then, just over a year after victory at Orléans, Joan rode into Compiégne in what would become her final battle. For some time, the French army had seemed to falter on occasion. With Joan at the helm, they had failed to capture Paris, and some of the king's advisors had even begun to question whether Joan's favor with God was growing thin. On May 23, 1430, Joan was captured in Compiégne by French-Burgundian soldiers loyal to the English. The Burgundians held her for months before negotiating a sale to the English. She spent more than a year in jail and stood trial for months.

Her crime? Heresy. For the English, it was imperative that Joan be proven to be a heretic. If they could not prove this, then it would mean that Joan was acting on God's behalf and that God himself was opposed to English rule of France. Political motivations, then, set the

stage for an ecclesiastical trial. Joan's status as a woman would be used to demonstrate this heresy at trial. Underlying every question was the disbelief that God could allow a woman—a girl!—to control an army, speak with saints, crown a king, and liberate French cities.

How, her interrogators would question again and again, could a young peasant girl really be acting under the direction of heavenly voices?

How could an insignificant young girl claim to receive heavenly help from the archangel Saint Michael, and from Saint Catherine and Saint Margaret? It was blasphemous for a girl to insist that she had been called of God. For a woman to wear men's clothing and cut her hair to appear like a man was proof that Joan was not led by God, they would argue, because God forbids such behavior. Joan was presented as a heretic and witch, crimes that were punishable by death if the accused would not repent.

Chapter Nine

There was also much at stake for France in Joan's trial, particularly for King Charles VII. For if Joan were proven to be a heretic and witch, it would invalidate the king's legitimacy and discredit his coronation. As such, Joan was left nearly abandoned during the long trial, in which a shrewd judge tried to trick her at every turn.[16] Joan, however, consistently responded with a sense of confidence, faith, and honor that has resonated through the pages of time. Her proceedings were one of the most thoroughly documented trials from the Medieval period, and many of her responses have lived on through history as a beacon of bravery.

When asked if she believed she was in God's grace, Joan responded, "If I am not, may God put me there; if I am, may God so keep me."[17]

When threatened with torture, even shown the instruments that would be used to inflict it, Joan replied, "Truly if you were to tear me limb from limb and separate my soul from my body, I would not tell you anything more: and if I did say anything, I should afterwards declare that you had compelled me to say it by force."[18]

When admonished to "correct and reform herself, her words and her deeds," Joan suggested that her interrogators first review her record and said, "then I will answer you. I trust in God my

creator for everything. I love Him with my whole heart."[19]

While awaiting trial and imprisoned in Beaulieu-lés-Fontaines, Joan had attempted to escape and was thus moved to a more northern castle, in Beaurevoir, farther from French lines. In the tower at Beaurevoir, the young maid had become desperate enough to attempt another, more risky escape. Despite her saints warning her not to, she had jumped sixty feet from the top of her prison tower. She was not seriously hurt, only unconscious and bruised. When questioned about the jump and its aftermath, she said, "I knew that I had been sold to the English, and I would have preferred to die rather than to be in the hands of the English, my enemies. . . . I was so wounded in that jump that I could neither eat nor drink; but nevertheless, I had comfort from St. Catherine."[20]

Chapter Ten

Joan was found guilty and sentenced to death by fire—a death that would later be viewed as evil and sacrilegious by many.

On May 30, 1431, Joan was taken to a public marketplace, tied to a pole, and set ablaze. Above the onlookers and crowd, an ally held up a cross for her to look upon, "so that the cross on which God hung during His life could be continually before her sight."[21] As the fire consumed her, she gazed up to heaven,

believing to the end that she would be with her God in paradise. Her last documented words were, "Jesus, Jesus, Jesus!"

Legend tells that at the very moment Joan of Arc bowed her head in death, a white dove emerged from the fire's flames and ascended into the heavens' bright lights and the loving arms of Joan's beloved saints, who welcomed her to paradise.

Chapter Eleven

The widespread reaction among many people of that time and place was that a great wrong and injustice had been done to Joan, the Maid of France. In fact, her execution did nothing to further England's attempts at victory in the still-raging war. Twenty-two years after Joan's death, when the war finally came to an end, England was expelled from France. A short time later, several inquests were opened concerning Joan's trial. In 1456, the trial and sentence were annulled and declared unjust and deceptive. Joan's name was cleared! Centuries later, Joan of Arc was canonized and became the patron Saint of France.

Apply What You Learned

Joan's faith in herself, God, and her angelic helpers inspired many to believe in themselves. Word spread, hope was kindled, and, before long soldiers, countrymen, and royalty flocked to her. They rallied beneath her banner and began fighting for independence.

Like Joan, we can trust that our lives have purpose. Like Joan, our faith can inspire others to rise and have hope despite overwhelming odds and challenges.

When Joan first set out for Chinon, with six men as her escort, to tell the Dauphin about her visions, she was asked, "How can you make such a journey when on all sides are soldiers?" Her response: "I do not fear the soldiers, for my road is made open to me; and if the soldiers come, I have God, my Lord, who will know how to clear the route. . . . It was for this that I was born."[22]

What were you born to do that inspires hope in others?

Film Notes

From the narrator of the companion film:

"While living in France as a child, we were taught about Joan of Arc. Many of these highlights of her life were already known to me, while a few others were not. I was unaware that she never used her sword to kill anyone. That is interesting to me because it shows that she most likely could have been protected by a higher power or her angels. I have a great deal of respect for Joan because she was true to herself and did not falter from her beliefs."

We asked the actress who portrays Joan in this book's companion film several questions about her experience. These are her responses.

Q: What is something you learned about Joan of Arc that you did not know before?
A: "Before the film I only knew that she was the patron saint of France and that she was burned at the stake. I did not know how young she was. I was impressed by her drive to complete the mission that her angels told her to do."

Q: How can people relate nowadays to Joan of Arc?
A: "Even though she lived over six hundred years ago, one of the ways we can relate to her

Jenna Adams as Joan of Arc

now is with the support systems that we have in our lives. If Joan did not have the support from her community and eventually the Dauphin, she would not have been able to liberate France. I think we can learn about the importance of our communities and how to build each other up to create a better society."

Q: Do you think Joan's destiny was pre-determined?
A: "Yes. Beforehand, it was prophesied that a maiden would come to save France, and then she came. You don't read about that a lot in literature, where a woman is prophesied to help and do something. For me as a woman, I was glad to read that France was looking for a woman to come and liberate them and that they were ready to receive her."

Stained Glass Window - Panel One by Todd Powelson

Stained Glass Window - Panel Two by Todd Powelson

Stained Glass Window - Panel Three by Todd Powelson

Timeline of Joan of Arc's Life

1412 - Joan of Arc born

1415 - Henry V of England attacks France

1425 - Joan first hears heavenly voices

1428 - Joan leaves home to help Charles VII become king

1429 - Liberates Orléans from the English;

      Charles VII crowned King of France

1430 - Joan Captured by English

1431 - Joan's trial begins;

      Joan burned at stake by English on May 30, 1431

1455 - Joan's family petitions for new trial

1456 - Catholic church overturns guilty verdict

1920 - Catholic church declares Joan a Saint

Timeline of World Events

1337 - Hundred Years' War begins between England and France

1413 - Henry V becomes King of England

1415 - Pope Gregory XII resigns

1420 - Brunelleschi begins work on the Duomo in Florence, Italy

1420 - Forbidden City finished in China

1427 - First witch hunts start in Switzerland

1438 - Incas rule in Peru

1440 - Around this year, Johannes Guttenberg invents printing press

1451 - Christopher Columbus born in Italy

1453 - Hundred Years' War ends;

    Beginning of Renaissance era

References & Notes

1 See Régine Pernoud and Marie Véronique Clin, Joan of Arc: Her Story, translated by Jeremy duQuesnay Adams (New York: St. Martin's Press, 1998), 200–01.

2 See Pernoud, Joan of Arc: Her Story, 201.

3 See Helen Castor, Joan of Arc: A History (London: Faber and Faber, 2014), xvi–xvii.

4 The words here, of course, are not direct quotes but a summary of what Joan testified that the Saints said to her. See Andrew Lang, The Maid of France: Being the Story of the Life and Death of Jeanne d'Arc (London: Longmans, Green, and Company, 1913), 38–40; see also Francis C. Lowell, Joan of Arc (Boston: Houghton, Mifflin and Company, 1896), 28.

5 See Lang, The Maid of France, 77; see also Castor, Joan of Arc, 99.

6 In Lowell, Joan of Arc, 57.

7 Joan's first meeting with the Dauphin—the future king of France—has become the stuff of legend. Neither Joan's testimony of the events nor those from several who were present in the hall at Chinon corroborate all of the elaborate details that have since been passed down regarding the meeting. (Some claimed that the king was in disguise, others said the king wasn't in the hall at all but entered later, and still others described several men in the crowd who pretended to be the

Dauphin.) But, as one of Joan's biographers writes, "One thing seems beyond doubt. Whatever circumstances caused the legend of the first encounter between dauphin and maid to swell into a theatrical set piece, Joan did not allow herself to be disconcerted by the intimidating spectacle of this great hall rustling with the whispers of high society and ablaze with a brightness to which she was unaccustomed. She went straight to the dauphin and calmly delivered the message for which she had crossed half the country" (Pernoud, Joan of Arc: Her Story, 23).

8 In Lowell, Joan of Arc, 67; see also Régine Pernoud, Joan of Arc: By Herself and Her Witnesses, translated by Edward Hyams (Lanham, MD: Scarborough House, 1994), 55–56.

9 See Lowell, Joan of Arc, 47; Castor, Joan of Arc, 86.

10 See Daniel Hobbins, trans., The Trial of Joan of Arc (Cambridge: Harvard University Press, 2005), 67; Pernoud, Joan of Arc: By Herself and Her Witnesses, 60–62; Lowell, Joan of Arc, 74–75; Castor, Joan of Arc, 100.

11 See Hobbins, The Trial of Joan of Arc, 69, 150.

12 In Pernoud, Joan of Arc: Her Story, 115.

13 In Pernoud, Joan of Arc: Her Story, 46.

14 In Pernoud, Joan of Arc: Her Story, 47.

15 In Willard Trask, trans., Joan of Arc: In Her Own Words (New York: Books & Co., 1996), 27.

16 One of her biographers writes that "No documentary evidence suggests that the king offered a ransom or made any effort whatsoever to free Joan of Arc. Although the English government was active, and spared neither time nor money, the king of France seemed stricken with complete inertia in regard to a ransom for Joan" (Pernoud, Joan of Arc: Her Story, 98).

17 W. P. Barrett, trans., The Trial of Jeanne D'arc: Translated into the English from the Original Latin and French Documents (Gotham House, Inc., 1932), 52, available online at https://sourcebooks.fordham.edu/basis/joanofarc-trial.asp. See also Pernoud, Joan of Arc: Her Story, 111–12.

18 In Barrett, The Trial of Jeanne D'arc, 302–3. See also Pernoud, Joan of Arc: Her Story, 127.

19 In Barrett, The Trial of Jeanne D'arc, 292. See also Pernoud, Joan of Arc: By Herself and Her Witnesses, 204.

20 In Pernoud, Joan of Arc: Her Story, 96.

21 Pernoud, Joan of Arc: Her Story, 136.

22 In Albert Bigelow Paine, Joan of Arc: Maid of France, Volume 1 (New York: The Macmillan Company, 1925), 48.

Bibliography

Brooks, Polly Schoyer, Beyond the Myth: The Story of Joan of Arc, Houghton Mifflin, Boston, 1999

Castor, Helen, Joan of Arc: A History, Harper Perennial; Illustrated edition, New York, 2016

Twain, Mark, Personal Recollections of Joan of Arc, Mark Twain's Collector's Edition, Jazzybee Verlag, Germany, 2017

Twain, Mark, Joan of Arc, Ignatius Press, San Francisco, First Edition, 1989

Demi, Joan of Arc, Cavendish, Tarrytown, NY, 2011

Hodges, Margaret, Joan of Arc: The Lily Maid, Holiday House, New York, 1999

North, Wyatt, Joan of Arc: A Life Inspired, Independently published, 2019

Pernoud, Regine, Joan of Arc: By Herself and Her Witnesses, Scarborough House, Lanham, MD, 1994

Pickels, Dwayne E., Women of Achievement: Joan of Arc, Chelsea House Publishers, Philadelphia, 2002

Watch For More Books, Videos & Podcasts From Awake Stories at
www.AWAKESTORIES.com

Abraham Lincoln

Alexander Hamilton

Harriet Tubman

George Washington

Frederick Douglass

Sacagawea

Adam Smith

Anne Frank

Benjamin Franklin

Queen Elizabeth I

Michelangelo

Mary The Mother

Marcus Aurelius

Mary Magdalene

Isaiah

Jane Austen

About the Author

Tara Mayoros is an author of several books with many more on the way, screenwriter, set designer, talent scout, business woman, master gardener, plant lady, artist, and DIYer. Her work has been featured from Disney to HGTV and many places in between.

When in need of inspiration, she heads to the mountains to either snow ski or water ski with her husband and children.

Diet Dr. Pepper and Indian food are her weaknesses. Finding incredible talent to work with, and seeing possibilities and potential in everything, are her strengths.

About the Artist

Todd Powelson, an artist, illustrator, and graphic designer, spends his time wandering through local canyons and up surrounding mountains, watching the trees, animals, and stars.

The natural world is often reflected in his work through mythology and archetype. He often uses pure color and cubist geometry to celebrate form, structure, and beauty.

Notes

Notes

Available Now From Awake Stories!

Available Now From Awake Stories!

Coming Soon From Awake Stories!

Coming Soon From Awake Stories!

Made in United States
Troutdale, OR
08/20/2024

22194238R00061